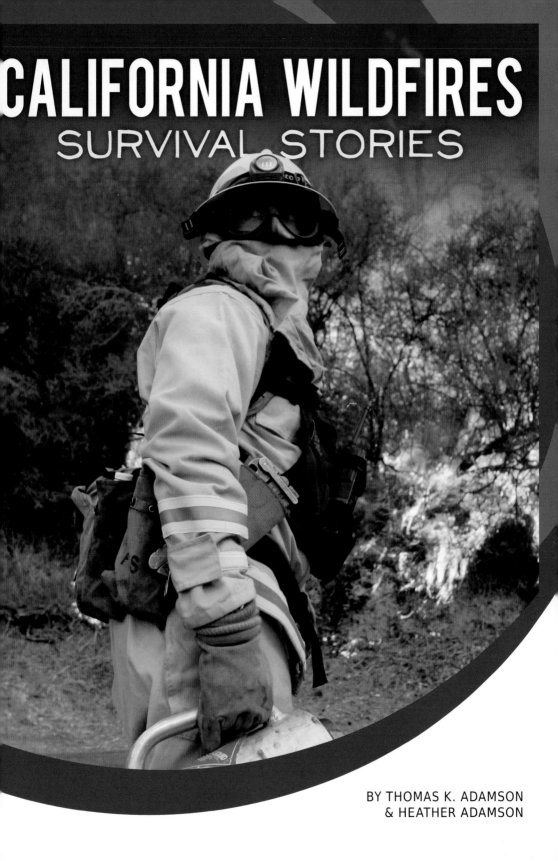

CALIFORNIA WILDFIRES
SURVIVAL STORIES

BY THOMAS K. ADAMSON
& HEATHER ADAMSON

The Child's World®
childsworld.com

Published by The Child's World®
1980 Lookout Drive • Mankato, MN 56003-1705
800-599-READ • www.childsworld.com

Acknowledgments
The Child's World®: Mary Berendes, Publishing Director
Red Line Editorial: Design, editorial direction, and production
Photographs ©: Mark J. Terrill/AP Images, cover, 1; Mike Meadows/ZumaPress/
Newscom, 6; Lenny Ignelzi/AP Images, 8; Crissy Pascual/U-T San Diego/ZumaPress/
Newscom, 10; Axel Koester/Corbis, 12; iStockphoto, 15 (foreground), 15 (background);
Chris Carlson/AP Images, 16, 26; Shutterstock Images, 19; Damian Dovarganes/AP
Images, 20; Nicolaus Czarnecki/ZumaPress/Corbis, 22; Ruaridh Stewart/ZumaPress/
Corbis, 24; Jon Mullen/iStockphoto, 25

ISBN 9781634074223

LCCN 2015946317

Printed in the United States of America
PA02353

ABOUT THE AUTHORS
Thomas K. and Heather Adamson have both written many books for kids.
This husband-and-wife team enjoys writing together. When they are not
working, the couple likes to take hikes, watch movies, eat pizza, and, of
course, read. They live in South Dakota with their two sons.

TABLE OF
CONTENTS

DISASTER STRIKES

In October 2007, large wildfires burned through Southern California. The fires spread quickly and burned large areas of land in only a matter of days. The fires moved quickly, but the conditions that led to the fires had been building for almost a year.

California was unusually dry in the winter of 2006 to 2007. The **drought** caused much vegetation in the region to die. Branches and sticks fell to the ground and could easily **ignite**. In January 2007, an unusual cold spell killed even more vegetation.

The drought continued throughout the summer. In fall, the Santa Ana winds began to kick in. These warm, dry winds can gust up to 70 to 80 miles per hour (113–129 km/h). The strong winds caused humidity to drop, making the already dry air even drier.

In the fall of 2007, fire risk in Southern California was very high. On October 21, eight fires started within hours of one another. Within days, more than 3,000 homes were destroyed, and hundreds were damaged. More than 500,000 acres (202,343 ha) burned. Hundreds of thousands of people had to **evacuate** their homes. Seventeen people died, and 140 firefighters were injured.

Despite the speed with which the fires spread, workers saved thousands of homes, and most people survived. Many made it through the fires by using lessons they had learned from wildfires that devastated the region in 2003.

FAST FACTS

Dates
• October 20, 2007 to October 31, 2007

Number of Fires
• 20

Total Area Burned
• 517,937 acres (209,602 ha)

Number of People Who Died
• 17

Number of Injuries
• 140 firefighters

Damage
• 3,069 homes and other buildings destroyed

Chapter 1

A TEAM EFFORT

At 11:00 a.m. on October 21, 2007, the fire station in Dulzura, California, received a call. The station's crew learned that wildfires were spreading rapidly through nearby areas struck by drought. The firefighters were asked to help protect buildings from the growing Harris fire. Firefighter Brooke Linman and her crew jumped into action. She rode Engine 3387 southeast toward Potrero, California, which is located near the Mexican border.

As the four firefighters neared their destination, small fires already burned beside the road. Engine 3387 drove through falling ash. Soon, the firefighters saw the trailer home they were called to protect. The home was already burning. A father and his young son were outside, frantic. It was too late to save the building, and the fire was moving in from the hillsides. Thick smoke began to fill the air, and **cinders** rained down around the crew.

◄ **A fire truck passes close to a blazing wildfire in Southern California on October 21, 2007.**

▲ Helicopter pilot Mike Wagstaff made a daring landing to save stranded firefighters and a young boy.

The firefighters tried to back the fire truck out, but the road was too narrow to turn around. The house fire flared. The heat from the blast stalled the fire truck and blew out its windows. The firefighters crawled out of the truck. They found cover behind some rocks with the boy. Linman deployed her emergency shelter. The tent-like covering is designed to protect against extreme heat. Linman brought the boy underneath the covering.

Air traffic controller Ray Chaney heard the radio call that the crew members were trapped by flames. Then, he heard them scream over the line. "We're burned over!" the voice on the line said. "We need help!"[1] Chaney called for any fire helicopters in the area to quickly come look for the crew. Pilot Mike Wagstaff was the first to spot them. He flew through smoke and flames and made a risky landing that was just long enough for the firefighters and the boy to climb on board. The father had not survived the flames. The helicopter rose out of the burning area and headed toward a safe landing zone.

Firefighter Matt Streck was in the area and heard the call for help. He got the attention of some **paramedics**. He knew the firefighters on the helicopter would need medical attention as soon as possible. Streck led the paramedics to the helicopter's landing spot. Walls of flames lined the road as they traveled. As the helicopter was touching down, the medical team arrived to help.

All of the crew of Engine 3387 suffered injuries. "We had worked together, and I couldn't recognize them," Streck said.[2]

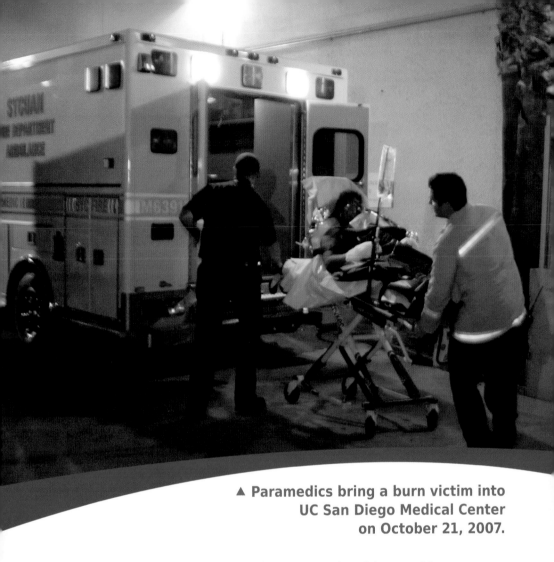

▲ Paramedics bring a burn victim into
UC San Diego Medical Center
on October 21, 2007.

Linman's were the worst. Her face, ears, shoulder, and lungs were badly burned. She knew it was bad. She thought she was going to die.

Doctors put Linman into a coma until November 4, hoping her body would heal. It worked. Linman survived. Community members and the governor of California later honored Linman for her heroic rescue of the boy.

WORST WILDFIRES IN CALIFORNIA HISTORY

Fierce winds helped make the Witch and Harris fires of October 2007 among the most destructive in California's history.

Fire Name	Date	Structures Lost	Deaths
Tunnel	October 1991	2,900	25
Cedar	October 2003	2,820	15
Witch	October 2007	1,650	2
Old	October 2003	1,003	6
Jones	October 1999	954	1
Paint	June 1990	641	1
Fountain	August 1992	636	0
Sayre	November 2008	604	0
City of Berkeley	September 1923	584	0
Harris	October 2007	548	8

Chapter 2

THE CASTLE FALLS

ost days, living in a castle in the hills of Malibu, California, would be a dream. Castle Kashan was set high in Malibu Canyon. Visitors could step out behind the home and look up at the mountains. Out of the front windows, they could look out and see the blue waters of the Pacific Ocean. This $17 million home hosted fancy weddings and celebrity parties.

But on the morning of October 21, 2007, visitor Daniel Collins looked out his bedroom window to a different scene. Thick, black smoke had turned the sky dark. "Quite a way to wake up," he said later.[3] He knew a fire must be close.

The fire was burning in the valley below the castle. The powerful Santa Ana winds had blown over three utility poles during the night. The power lines had sparked as they fell. The dry land quickly flamed up. Even though the castle was not in

◄ People in Malibu, California, were forced to evacuate on October 21, 2007, as fire spread through nearby hills.

the wildfire's direct path, strong, whipping winds had carried a burning cinder far up the hill. The castle was burning.

Lilly Lawrence, the castle's owner, was also home. She saw the fire, too. She knew there would be only moments to grab a few things and get out. The castle was filled with valuables: **antiques**, artwork, autographs of world leaders, a prized Elvis Presley collection, and more. Collins and Lawrence filled their arms with valuables as the firefighters arrived.

Meanwhile, the fire climbed the castle walls. Giant bricks began to fall. Firefighters carried some valuables as they helped Collins and Lawrence leave the castle. One carried photos of U.S. presidents. Lawrence hauled out Elvis Presley's army uniforms. They did not have time to take anything else. The important thing was for everyone to reach safety, which they did.

The stone and wood castle burned to the ground. Television helicopters filmed the fire. People watched the Malibu landmark and its valuables go up in flames. Lawrence tried not to be too upset. "My parents taught me not to allow my possessions to possess me," she told reporters. "The house is a house."[4] The Canyon fire burned 4,521 acres (1,830 ha). It wrecked dozens of homes and a church.

MAP OF THE BLAZES

Twenty fires broke out across Southern California, starting on October 20, 2007. This map shows each fire's starting location and the order in which the fires ignited.

3. Sedgewick

1. Ranch

7. Buckweed

17. Magic

13. Grass Valley

12. Cajon

8. Nightsky

5. October

15. Slide

2. Canyon

10. Santiago

18. Rosa

9. Roca

20. Ammo

19. Poomacha

16. Rice

11. McCoy

14. Coronado Hills

6. Witch

4. Harris

Chapter 3

A FIREPROOF HOME

On October 21, Lisa LeFors received the news over the radio. The strong Santa Ana winds were bringing fire toward her home in Ramona, California. The winds had stoked the flames so much that firefighters could not contain them. The blaze that was headed toward Ramona was part of the Witch fire, the biggest of the 2007 wildfires.

As the fire approached, LeFors prepared to evacuate. But unlike many residents, she did not pack her valuables into her car. She was not worried about her home or her possessions within it. The building was built to resist fires. The walls were made of brick. The roof consisted of concrete tiles. The outside doors were metal, and the windows had metal frames. Everything was designed to keep fire from entering the house.

A small wall along the patio provided further protection. On the other side of the wall, the main vegetation was ice plant.

◀ **Gusting winds spread a wildfire through Ramona, California, on October 22, 2007.**

This type of plant holds a lot of moisture and grows low to the ground, making it fire resistant.

LeFors was confident the ice plant and wall would keep the fire away from her house. But she was worried about a propane tank 30 feet (9 m) away. If the fire reached the tank, it could explode. So before she left, LeFors removed a pile of leaves from under the tank. Then, at 2:00 a.m., she evacuated with her two dogs and one cat. She believed her house would be safe, but she did not want to take any chances. The Santa Ana winds were blowing hard. "I've never seen a wind like that," LeFors said.[5]

When LeFors returned, she saw that one of her neighbor's homes had burned completely to the ground. At her house, she found cinders from the fire on windowsills. The metal frames had prevented them from igniting the house. The ground surrounding her home was scorched up to the ice plant. The ice plant had also protected the propane tank, which was still intact. LeFors was pleased to find no damage. According to her neighbor, who had stayed during the fire, the area burned for about two hours before moving on.

In other homes and neighborhoods with fire-resistant measures in place, residents reported similar results. In many, it looked like the fire just stopped at the edge of the properties.

With planning and technology, these homeowners proved that houses could be made fireproof.

DEFENSIBLE SPACE

People can create spaces around their homes that minimize the risk of fire spreading to the structures.

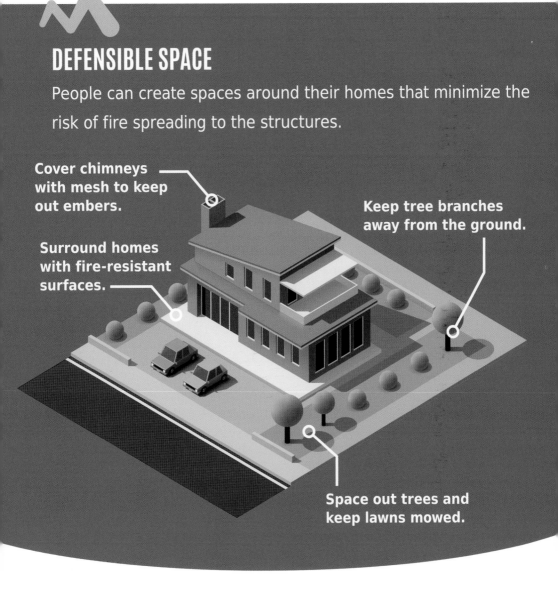

Cover chimneys with mesh to keep out embers.

Keep tree branches away from the ground.

Surround homes with fire-resistant surfaces.

Space out trees and keep lawns mowed.

Chapter 4

A NARROW ESCAPE

On October 22, reserve firefighter Marc Grossman and his crew were fighting the Santiago fire near Irvine, California. They were working from a road in the base of a valley. The fire burned on one side of the road. Hundreds of homes sat on the other side. The firefighters were trying to keep the fire from crossing the road and reaching the homes.

The wind started out in the firefighters favor. But then, it suddenly shifted. The fire crossed the road and started to spread across the hillside. Grossman and members of other crews went up the hillside to try to put out the flames that had crossed the road. They made little progress. Fire burst their hose, making them unable to fight the fire. Flames shot up the hillside toward the firefighters. The blaze had spread to three sides of the hill and was climbing up toward their position. The other side of the hill dropped steeply toward the road. Grossman and the 11 other

◀ **A wildfire approaches homes in Santiago Canyon on October 23, 2007.**

firefighters were surrounded. They were trapped near the top of the hill with no water to protect them.

The firefighters had no time to move away from the flames. "Let's make a run for it," one of the firefighters suggested.[6] But there was nowhere to run. Their only option was to get inside their portable shelters. These sleeping-bag-sized shelters look like aluminum foil. They are designed to reflect heat.

Grossman was training a new firefighter. It was her first fire. He told her to stay with him and to do what he did. "I need you to deploy your fire shelter," he said.[7]

They threw the shelters over their heads and crawled inside. They then dropped to the ground and held the sides down. The fire roared near them. It was hot and hard to breathe inside the shelters. They could hear the fire crackling outside.

The fire captain on the scene tried to radio for help. "Can you get a helicopter over here?"[8]

He did not get the response he was looking for. "Negative. We do not have air support available."[9]

Because of all the other fires going on, helicopters could not get there right away. The firefighters were now in danger.

The fire captain said, "We just had a shelter deployment!"

◄ **Firefighters must be careful never to be surrounded by a fire.**

"A shelter deployment?"

"Yes, a shelter deployment on the ridge line."

"Copy that."[10]

Now, all the firefighters could do was wait. While they were inside, Grossman and the firefighter-in-training could hear each other through the walls of their shelters. Grossman told her, "Your dad is going to kill me!" She joked back, "Well, my sister's going to kill you also."[11]

After 12 long minutes, helicopters finally arrived to dump water on the fire. Right away, the firefighters could feel their shelters cool down. After a few minutes, they got out of their shelters. No one was hurt. They saw the hillside was now completely burned. Another crew was approaching from below with chainsaws. They were cutting a path through the burned material so the 12 firefighters on the hill could get down.

After getting checked out by medical personnel, Grossman and the firefighter-in-training went back to work fighting more fires.

HELITANKER

The Erickson Air-Crane is a 70-foot (21-m) long helicopter designed for fighting fires and moving heavy objects. The helicopter can lift up to 20,000 pounds (9,072 kg).

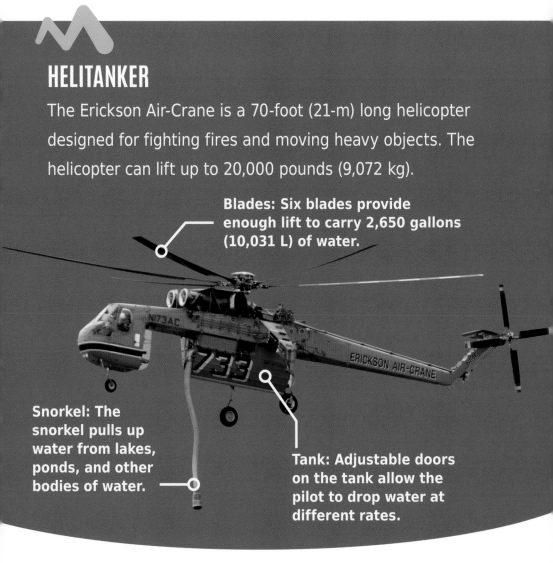

Blades: Six blades provide enough lift to carry 2,650 gallons (10,031 L) of water.

Snorkel: The snorkel pulls up water from lakes, ponds, and other bodies of water.

Tank: Adjustable doors on the tank allow the pilot to drop water at different rates.

Chapter 5

A CITY OF CARING

As fire approached their neighborhood in Ramona, California, Nadar and Leticia Hamdan evacuated their home. They packed their family into their motor home and drove away. Like many others in the area, the family went to Qualcomm Stadium. The stadium normally hosts the San Diego Chargers football team. But because of the fires, about 9,000 people temporarily settled in and around the building.

Twenty-four-year-old Josue De Los Diaz did not go to the stadium because his house was in danger. He kept thinking about the people who could not sleep in their own beds because of the fires. De Los Diaz went to Qualcomm to **volunteer**. He spent his day off from work sorting blankets and putting cots together. And he was not the only one who wanted to help.

Volunteers flooded in from around the state. They partnered with local businesses to think of everything they could do for the

◄ **Thousands of people flocked to the home of the San Diego Chargers football team seeking relief from the California wildfires.**

displaced residents. Free concerts, magicians, massages, crafts, games, and computers with Internet were all provided to the people staying at the stadium. Buffets of gourmet food, piles of snacks, and towers of cartons of drinks ensured that no one was hungry. Blankets, sleeping bags, tents, cots, and pillows gave each person a place to sleep. The air-conditioned suites on the upper levels turned into a nursing home for about 500 elderly people. It was staffed with doctors and nurses. An on-site pharmacy was set up with donated medicine. The stadium turned into a little city. There were clothes, toothbrushes, diapers—anything someone who was not at home might need.

Ester Francis, 91, appreciated the caring, carnival-like atmosphere. After fleeing her own home to stay with her son, the fire forced them to leave there, too. A couple of cots in the football field's end zone were their beds for now. "Everyone's so friendly," Francis said. "I guess it's making us all feel secure at a time when we all feel so insecure."[12] The Hamdans seemed to feel the same. When they learned their home was totally gone, they signed up as volunteers. They passed out soap and supervised kids in the play area. They lost a home but still felt like part of a great community.

FIRE ENGINES SENT BY STATE

Many western and midwestern states sent fire engines to help battle the October 2007 California wildfires.

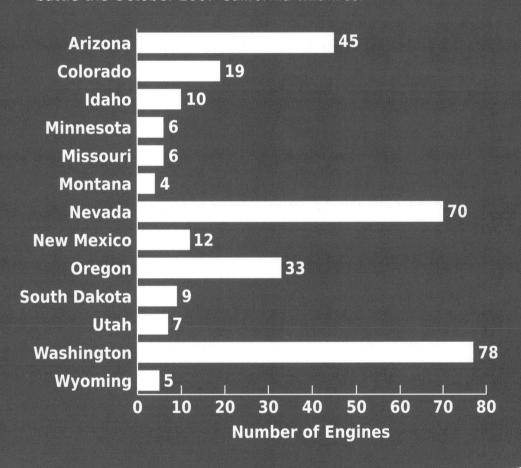

State	Number of Engines
Arizona	45
Colorado	19
Idaho	10
Minnesota	6
Missouri	6
Montana	4
Nevada	70
New Mexico	12
Oregon	33
South Dakota	9
Utah	7
Washington	78
Wyoming	5

Number of Engines

GLOSSARY

antiques (an-TEEKS): Antiques are old and valuable objects. People carried antiques out of Castle Kashan before it burned.

cinders (SIN-durz): Small pieces of wood that have been partly burned are cinders. Cinders can fly across roads and spread fire.

drought (drout): A drought is a long period with little or no rain. A drought can increase the likelihood of a fire breaking out.

evacuate (i-VAK-yoo-ate): To evacuate is to move away from a dangerous area. People living in areas threatened by wildfire often evacuate days in advance.

ignite (ig-NITE): To ignite is to catch on fire. Ice plants do not ignite easily.

paramedics (par-uh-MED-iks): Paramedics are people trained to care for others in emergencies. Paramedics helped treat burn victims during the wildfires.

volunteer (vah-luhn-TEER): To volunteer is to work without pay. Many people came to Qualcomm Stadium to volunteer to help those affected by wildfire.

SOURCE NOTES

1. Associated Press. "Firefighter Heroics Saved 4 from Calif. Blazes." *NBCNews.com*. NBC Universal, 10 Oct. 2007. Web. 10 Jun. 2015.

2. Ibid.

3. Daniel Collins. "Transcript: Malibu Fires Continue to Burn." *CNN*. Turner Broadcasting System, Inc., 21 Oct. 2007. Web. 10 Jun. 2015.

4. Dan Glaister. "Hollywood Flees as Wildfires Sweep Coast of California." *The Guardian*. Guardian News, 22 Oct. 2007. Web. 10 Jun. 2015.

5. California. Governor's Office of Emergency Services. "Defensible Space and Fire-Resistant Building Materials Save Home from Wildfire." *Southern California Best Practices*. OES California, Feb. 2008. Web. 10 Jun. 2015.

6. Steve Concialdi. "Santiago Fire." *Wildland Fire Lessons Learned Center*. National Park Service, 19 Mar. 2014. Web. 10 Jun. 2015.

7. Marc Grossman. "Transcript: 2007 Santiago Fire." *Center for Oral and Public History*. California State University, Fullerton, 21 Jun. 2008. Web. 10 Jun. 2015.

8. Bryan Chan. "Santiago Fire Shelter Deployment." *LA Times*. Los Angeles Times, 22 Oct. 2007. Web. 10 Jun. 2015.

9. Ibid.

10. Ibid.

11. Marc Grossman. "Transcript: 2007 Santiago Fire." *Center for Oral and Public History*. California State University, Fullerton, 21 Jun. 2008. Web. 10 Jun. 2015.

12. Scott Lindlaw. "At Qualcomm Stadium Evacuation Center, Massages and Buffets Lift Spirits." *KPBS*. KPBS Public Broadcasting, 23 Oct. 2007. Web. 10 Jun. 2015.

TO LEARN MORE

Books

Furgang, Kathy. *Wildfires*. Washington, DC: National Geographic Children's Books, 2015.

Mara, Wil. *Smokejumper*. Ann Arbor, MI: Cherry Lake Publishing, 2015.

Mason, Paul. *Wildfires*. Mankato, MN: Smart Apple Media, 2012.

Web Sites

Visit our Web site for links about the 2007 California wildfires: childsworld.com/links

Note to Parents, Teachers, and Librarians: We routinely verify our Web links to make sure they are safe and active sites. So encourage your readers to check them out!

INDEX